The FACT ATTACK series

Awesome Aliens
Beastly Bodies
Cool Cars
Crazy Creatures
Crucial Cricket
Dastardly Deeds
Deadly Deep
Devastating Dinosaurs
Dreadful Disasters
Fantastic Football
Gruesome Ghosts
Incredible Inventions
Mad Medicine
Magnificent Monarchs
Nutty Numbers
Remarkable Rescues
Rowdy Rugby
Spectacular Space
Super Spies
Vile Vampires

FACT ATTACK

IAN LOCKE

MACMILLAN CHILDREN'S BOOKS

First published 1999 by Macmillan Children's Books

This edition published 2012 by Macmillan Children's Books
a division of Macmillan Publishers Limited
20 New Wharf Road, London N1 9RR
Basingstoke and Oxford
Associated companies throughout the world
www.panmacmillan.com

ISBN 978-1-4472-2444-0

1 3 5 7 9 8 6 4 2

A CIP catalogue record for this book is available from
the British Library.

Printed and bound by CPI Group (UK) Ltd, Croydon CR0 4YY

DID YOU KNOW THAT . . .

The first mystery of the area which became known as the Bermuda Triangle happened in 1902, when the German cargo ship *Freya* was found abandoned and crewless.

At least 21 species of shark live in British waters, including the basking shark, the world's second largest fish, which can grow to a length of 15 metres.

4,000 sharks were caught off Britain in 1971.

A famous 'ghost ship' was found in the Bermuda Triangle in October 1944. The only living thing aboard the *Rubicon*, a Cuban freighter, was a dog – and the only signs that something had happened were a broken rope and a missing lifeboat. During that month a ferocious hurricane had swept the area. The ship may have begun to drift and, in a panic, the captain and crew may have taken to a lifeboat. If they did, they would have perished in the storm.

 Seals have been known to swim great distances. In April 1998 a bearded seal was found exhausted and hungry on the beach at Mablethorpe, Lincolnshire. After it had been rescued and named Whiskers, it was discovered that it had swum all the way from Greenland. The last time a bearded seal had been seen in Britain was in 1892, on the Norfolk coast.

The most shark-infested coast in the USA is that of Northern California. It is nicknamed the Red Triangle.

 One-time Chelsea defender Frank Leboeuf survived an ordeal by sharks on 2 August 1997.

 The US diving manual lists all sorts of sea creatures as dangerous. One of the strangest of these is the giant clam, which, we are told, can trap people's arms and legs, holding them until they drown. There is, however, no record of anyone drowning after being trapped by a clam.

 Baby sharks begin to hunt on their own as soon as they are born.

There are two types of whale: toothed whales and whalebone whales. Whalebone is an elastic horny substance which grows in a series of thin strips in the upper jaw of some whales instead of teeth. It is often used to stiffen parts of dresses.

 The deep-sea octopus, found off the Alaskan coast, can grow up to 10 metres long.

 Along a shark's body there is a series of sensory organs which detect movement in the water. If a person splashes or thrashes in the water, the shark often assumes it is a crippled or wounded body. The best protection from attack is to move slowly in the water and stay in the same position.

The ocean can be up to seven miles (11 km) deep. It is easier to get information from the surface of the moon than from the depths of the ocean.

 The poison-box jellyfish is so poisonous that rescuers of people stung by it have been known to die after touching the poison tentacles still in a victim's skin. People stung look like they have been whipped.

 In 1990 Leo Kennedy caught a 460-kg man-eating shark off the island of Mauritius. It took him over four hours to haul it in. The news of his catch reached the famous London store Harrods and Mohamed Al-Fayed, the store's owner, paid for the shark to be brought to England and put on display in Harrods. It was given the name Tiny, after Mr Al-Fayed's business rival 'Tiny' Rowland. Some time later the shark was sold for charity.

Fish don't chew their food – they haven't the time! They need to use the gills in the walls of their mouths non-stop to breathe.

 If the water in the sea were to evaporate it has been calculated that the layer of salt left behind would be seven metres thick.

 Off Monterey Bay, California, there is a two-mile-deep canyon.

 A Japanese couple were swept out to sea on a blow-up dolphin in September 1997. They then survived 24 hours in shark-infested waters.

Though dolphins are intelligent, the smaller-toothed whale is rated the brightest sea creature.

 Cockles are unusual – they jump when attacked, sometimes leaping to a height of 20 centimetres!

 British soldiers suffering from trench foot during World War I used to rub whale oil on their feet.

 On 30 December 1947, when sailing through the Caribbean, the passenger liner *Santa Clara* reported running over an unidentified sea monster. It was said to be 14 metres long and 90 centimetres wide with a head like an eel.

The fastest fish in the world is the sailfish. It can reach a speed of 110 kph or 60 mph.

 One of the oddest sea creatures is the *Sarcophagus flagellum*. It looks like a long tube with a gaping mouth of sharp teeth and a long, whip-like tail. It grows to nearly two metres and lives in continual darkness, at great pressure and at a temperature below zero in the depths of the sea.

 A Greenland or right whale (so called by whalers because they were the right whales to catch) weighs the same as about five elephants.

 The robot machines used to explore at great depths are called ROVs, Remotely Operated Vehicles.

The blue whale can survive on its own blubber without eating for six months.

 The majority of sea creatures live between the surface of the sea and a depth of 200 metres.

 The fastest swimming sharks are the mako sharks and the blue sharks. They can reach speeds of between 22 mph and 60 mph.

 The lowest form of life, algae, appeared in the sea about 1,200 million years ago.

Bruce Mounier, a diver and photographer
from Miami, had an incredible experience
in 1968. He reported seeing an 'underwater
abominable snowman'. He said the
creature he saw had a monkey's face, with
large eyes and a long neck.

 Carp fish are a bit odd. A Thai carp,
Delilah, once kept at the Lobster
Tail restaurant near Luton, England,
had a diet of fruit and beans. Delilah
turned from grey to pink when she was
happy.

A porbeagle shark weighing a record
230 kg was caught off Dunnet Head in
the north of Scotland in August 1993.

An underwater concert was held in
memory of the great underwater explorer
Jacques Cousteau in July 1997. 650
musicians, wearing diving gear, played for
about six hours off Pine Key in Florida!

Ten of the best-known films to include
submarines have been:

1. *Mystery Submarine* (1953)
2. *Torpedo Alley* (1953)
3. *20,000 Leagues Under the Sea* (1954)
4. *The Enemy Below* (1957)
5. *Atomic Submarine* (1959)
6. *Voyage to the Bottom of the Sea* (1961)
7. *The Bedford Incident* (1965)
8. *Around the World Under the Sea* (1966)
9. *Yellow Submarine* (1968)
10. *Ice Station Zebra* (1969)

 In 1993 a Chinese man paid £47,000
for a goldfish.

There is a stretch of water off Japan which is known as the Devil or Ghost Sea because many ships and aircraft have disappeared there. It is Japan's Bermuda Triangle. The area is known for its sudden tidal waves and there have been reports of luminous or glowing white water and the sudden appearance of holes or hills in the sea.

 Old sailors believed that nails and hair should not be cut at sea except in a storm.

 Penguins have knees. These can be seen when they jump out of water.

 There were two sea monsters in the Bible, the Raha and the Leviathan.

Cod usually eat on the sea floor. They eat virtually anything. Bunches of keys, a hare, a white turnip, a leather-bound book and a long piece of candle have all been found in their stomachs. The acid in their stomachs is strong enough to dissolve seashells and the shells of crabs.

 The Australian devil fish is completely black and has a very gruesome face. It is also a heavyweight – it can weigh up to two tonnes!

 The largest squid on record was over 18 metres long.

Cod liver oil was used as a medicine as long ago as 1770. It wasn't until 1921 that it was proved to help cure rickets, the disease that makes bones thin, soft and fragile because of lack of vitamins.

Sharks can detect blood from a quarter of a mile away. They have two scent detectors on either side of their snout and can follow a scent trail from both sides, thereby homing in on prey.

The tenth rarest mammal on Earth is the Indus dolphin. There are only about 1,100 left.

When very hungry, sea lions will attack and eat pelicans.

A Royal Navy ship, the frigate HMS *Birkenhead*, crashed into a reef off the coast of South Africa on a wild night in 1852. There were 680 people aboard. A nightmare began. The women and children were sent off in a boat, but there were still 600 men left behind. As the ship lurched into the sea, many of the men were thrown into the waves. They were soon surrounded by a pack of sharks and were attacked. There were hundreds of sharks. The 200 men left aboard knew what was in store for them as the ship sank. Only 60 of the men made it to the shore alive. When the story of the ship's loss was made public, the Royal Navy made no mention of the gruesome shark attacks.

 In the 1960s it was predicted that people would soon live under the sea and create giant fish farms and bases for exploration . . .

During the voyage of the steamship *Valhalla* in 1905, two scientists from London Zoo, Edmund Meade-Waldo and Michael Nicholl, reported seeing a deep-sea monster off Brazil. They claimed it was about two metres long and about as thick as a human body. The monster soon disappeared beneath the waves. It was seen again about 14 hours later. The two men said it looked like a submarine just under the surface of the sea. What the creature actually was remains a mystery.

 The first serious voyage to study the deep ocean was made by the British ship *Challenger* in 1872. It investigated the deep sea and found thousands of creatures new to science.

On 29 June 1998, fisherman Douglas Chesser bled to death after being attacked by a shark off southern Australia. A local four-metre shark called Kong was suspected. It was the first fatal attack by a shark off southern Australia for seven years.

As the flatfish grows into an adult, it changes from swimming vertically to swimming horizontally. Its eyes change position, moving across the forehead so that both eyes are on the left.

The most famous of deep ocean stories, *20,000 Leagues Under the Sea*, by Jules Verne, was published in 1870.

Australian Brian Rodger was a
champion spear fisherman. In the
summer of 1961 he went in for a
big competition at a place called
Snapper Point in southern Australia.
Brian knew he had to be fit for the
competition, but he didn't know his
fitness was to save his life. After he'd
been underwater for a while, Brian
saw a chance to get a big shark.
Coming up briefly, he plunged
down again. But it was a great
white, nearly four metres long, and
unfortunately it got him instead! The
shark caught his leg, then crunched
his arm with a bite that came close
to the bone.

Brian poked his attacker in the
eyes. The shark went away briefly,
but with the scent of blood, it soon
came at him again. Brian launched

his spear into the creature, but, in moments, the great white had shaken it off. Brian swam for his life to a reef a kilometre away. He tied up his leg with rubber from his knife handle to stop the blood flow, threw off his lead belt, and dumped his spear gun and the line of fish he had caught for the competition.

Not far from the shore, he was reached by a couple of fishermen in a boat. He was rushed to hospital and needed about 200 stitches and seven pints of blood to save him. Despite his ordeal, Brian was not put off – he was out swimming again within twelve weeks!

Comb-jellies, which make their own light, look like swimming lanterns in the deep. They live at a depth of up to 3,000 metres.

 Like dinosaurs, sharks never lose their teeth. When they bite victims (people, fish or animals) and leave teeth behind, more teeth grow in their place.

 Frenchman Jacques Cousteau collected the original aqualung, a portable breathing apparatus for divers, from a railway station at Bandol, southern France, in 1943.

Fish and fishy creatures don't always live in the sea. Among the more unusual items found in the 212,500 miles of sewers in Britain in 1997 were sea trout, salmon and a salamander. The stranger items included a stuffed gorilla, a set of jail keys and a working Yamaha organ!

 William Beebe, an American from New York, was the first to explore the deep sea. He travelled half a mile down in 1936, locked in a steel ball. When he came back and told people about the strange and wonderful things he had seen, many did not believe him and thought he was imagining things.

 Each year the water level in the northern oceans drops. The missing water does not turn up in the southern oceans. What happens to it remains a mystery.

The starfish has an eye on the end of each of its arms.

 The shark is the only fish that can blink.

 Sharks have little sense of pain. Even when torn by an attacker, they will continue to fight.

 The modern king crab, found in the sea round America, is one of the oldest living creatures. It is the descendant of the trilobite, an ancient sea creature from the time of the dinosaurs.

 The giant squid has eyes that measure over 30 centimetres in diameter.

A special submarine, the *Deep Flight One*, was launched in 1997 to explore the bottom of the sea. It can descend to a depth of over 1.5 kilometres. Its design is based on that of a simple glider.

 Many of the creatures which live at a great depth are composed almost entirely of water.

 At great depth there is so much pressure that the two US subs *Thresher* and *Scorpion*, which were lost in the deep, were found to have been crushed like paper.

 In the deep ocean many creatures do not encounter solid surfaces. As a result they are very difficult to keep healthy in aquariums.

The common dolphin can only stay underwater for two to three minutes.

 Scientists in the USA have recorded the calls of many whales and other creatures. They have also recorded underwater earthquakes, which make a sound like rolling thunder.

 One of the most dangerous meals for a shark is the porcupine fish. This fish has hundreds of spines which will catch in the shark's throat, killing it.

The self-lighting fish, which can survive great pressure and lights up when thousands of metres below the sea, can also survive near the surface. How it manages to withstand the great change in pressure is unknown.

 Strange carpets can exist at sea. In the Sargasso Sea great stretches of the seaweed sargassum can come together and can sometimes be mistaken for land.

 The human being is basically not built for diving in deep water. The pressure underwater forces the body joints to grind together.

The needle fish is a freak. It is ten centimetres long and only a quarter of a centimetre thick!

 On the afternoon of 5 December 1945, five US planes had completed a US navy training exercise off a group of small islands near Bermuda. They began their return to their base at Fort Lauderdale, Florida, as a storm began to blow in. They never arrived. No trace of them could be found in the search that followed. The leading pilot, Lieutenant Charles Taylor, last reported that his compasses had failed. Nothing more was heard. The disappearance of Flight 19 was featured in Steven Spielberg's *Close Encounters of the Third Kind*, in which the pilots are abducted by aliens.

Seven types of sharks have been known to attack people:

1. The great white shark
2. The oceanic white-tip shark
3. The tiger shark
4. The mako shark
5. The bull shark
6. The hammerhead shark
7. The cookiecutter shark

The common dolphin has been seen surfing on the wake of ships, reaching speeds of over 39 kph or 24 mph!

Several 'ghost ships' appear to exist. During July 1975, Dr Jim Thorne, an American aboard the yacht *New Freedom*, heard a crack of thunder and saw flashes of lightning. The storm was so impressive he took some photographs. When the film was developed he got a surprise. On the edge of the pictures there was an image of an old-fashioned, square-rigged sailing ship! He was positive there were no ships close to him during the brief storm.

 The record-breaking diving vessel the *Trieste* could reach a depth of over six kilometres. It was named after the Italian city that financed it.

The iceberg that was hit by the *Titanic* on the historic night of 14–15 April 1912 had originally broken off from Greenland in 1909.

The oddest-looking shark is the goblin shark. Its face looks very wrinkled and ancient, and it has a long, rounded horn on its head, above an ugly blunt snout.

 Most shark attacks happen at the weekends because there are more people splashing and making noise on the seashore.

 It has recently been found that beaked whales suck in their food (mainly squid and fish) like a hoover.

 Some areas of the sea are almost immediately deadly. A person can survive a maximum of only ten minutes in the cold Labrador Current off Canada.

The smallest shark is the dwarf. It grows to only 15 cm.

 The first hatchling of a sand-tiger shark will eat all its other potential brothers and sisters (as eggs) before they are born!

 In July 1998 an American was three times more likely to be killed by a shark and one million times more likely to be murdered than to win the US lottery powerball jackpot of over $100 million.

 During the Cold War, the US put down listening devices called SOSAS across the world's oceans. It cost them $16 billion!

One of the worst shark attacks in the United States happened in a river! On 12 July 1916, twelve-year-old Lester Stillwell was swimming in the Matapan Creek, New Jersey, some 15 miles from the sea, when he was attacked by a great white shark. A friend came to his rescue but was also snapped up by the shark. Over the next ten days, four other people were killed in shark attacks along the coast. A great shark hunt began and eventually a 2.6-metre great white was caught in a net four miles from the creek.

 Zebra sharks are born with stripes but they turn spotty when they grow up.

In 1959, American teenager Shirley O'Neill went out with her boyfriend Albert Kogler. They planned to go swimming at Baker's Beach, California. When Shirley had not returned by eight that night, her mother became worried. She was just about to call Albert's house, when there was a visit to her door. On the step stood a policeman and, beside him, in a hospital gown, a pale and shivering Shirley. Shirley told her mother that Albert had been caught by a shark. When the shark attacked, Shirley swam out to Albert and grabbed him. She found his arm was almost bitten off. She had to hold him up as she swam for the shore. By sheer courage she wrestled Albert from the shark. She made it to the shore, but Albert died of his injuries in hospital. In 1960 her bravery was rewarded. President Kennedy awarded her the Young American People's Medal of Valor for her efforts to save Albert.

Most baby seals are born with a soft woolly coat of fur called lanugo. They lose it before they first go in the water.

 The skin of the angel shark was used by the Samurai warriors of Japan as a firm grip for the handles of their famous and often beautiful swords.

 The eyes of a shark glow in the dark like those of a cat.

 Fifty American whaling ships made the first journey to the Antarctic in 1767.

The Marianas Trench in the Pacific is so deep it would take an hour for an object to sink to the bottom.

 Under 10 per cent of sharks are dangerous to humans.

 David Bushnell pioneered the use of the submarine in warfare. His sub went into action on 6 September 1776 in New York Harbor. It was supposed to bore holes in British ships, put charges in the holes and blow them up. Since the main British ships had copper bottoms to protect them, it wasn't even possible to make the holes.

The humpback whale is so large it gets covered in barnacles. They have a clever way of getting rid of the little creatures. They go to a warm freshwater river where the barnacles cannot survive so drop off. Having noticed this, sailors used to put their ships into fresh water to remove the barnacles that encrusted the hulls.

 The first British submarine was launched at Barrow on 2 October 1901.

 Ice fish are some of the weirdest around. They live in the cold of the Antarctic and have no red blood. They survive on very little oxygen and their hearts are three times the size of red-blooded fish.

The great white shark has teeth which slice like a razor. A 300 kg fish can be cut in half in one bite!

 Some creatures of the deep are not quite what they seem. The wobbegong shark looks like a carpet. Its head is covered with a broad fringe. As a result of this camouflage the shark can sneak up on its prey.

 In June 1991, the treasure-hunting ship *Deep Sea*, sailing off the coast of Miami, Florida, made a weird find – five World War II bombers, neatly lined up together on the sea floor. The area was an old US bombing range and aircraft were often ditched in a line during the years 1943–5.

Joshua Slocum, an American, was the first man to sail alone around the world. He ended his three-year journey on 3 July 1898. Curiously, he never learned to swim.

 The skin of the whale shark is 10 cm thick. They have the thickest skin of any creature.

 Turtles have no teeth.

 The first shark was brought to England by the sailor and trader John Hawkins in 1569.

 A shark has been tracked over an amazing distance of 1,850 kilometres, from New York, America, to the Cape Verde islands off the west coast of Africa.

Seals normally live in the sea (or in zoos) but in 1951 one turned up in the famous Trevi fountain in Rome. It had been acquired by two Italian journalists on Sardinia and they decided it should have a swim in the fountain. A policeman arrived and fined them for putting the seal there. The seal was then taken out of the fountain, but it did not leave in a tank of water – it was driven off in a car!

 The ship of the English pirate Samuel Bellamy, the *Whydah*, loaded with 180 bags of treasure, sank in a storm off Cape Cod, Massachusetts, in 1717. Only two on board survived, including Welsh carpenter Thomas Davis who told the tale of the ship and its treasure. In July 1984, treasure hunter Barry Clifford found the wreck of the *Whydah* on the seabed. The recovery of the treasure continued until 1988. By the time Barry Clifford and his team had finished they had found a haul of treasure and items from the wreck that were valued at as much as $400 million – £275 million!

In May 1957 the US Air Force were able to accurately measure the exact width of the Atlantic Ocean (from Europe to North America) but said the information was secret!

 During World War II a number of killer whales were stranded around Britain. It is thought this was because of anti-submarine activities which disorientated them.

 During the summer the average temperature of the Red Sea (between Africa and Arabia) is 30°C – almost as warm as the average bath!

The world's most poisonous snake is found in the sea! It was named after the explorer Sir Edward Belcher in 1849 and its poison is a hundred times more deadly than that of the most venomous snake on land, the western taipan of Australia.

 A fibreglass robot shark was used in a test to frighten away unwanted visitors to beaches owned by millionaires in the USA in 1976.

 Dolphins sleep for only two hours a day.

 The killer whale will eat just about anything that swims – including other whales, dolphins, penguins, fish and squid. Once a pack has killed another whale they always eat the tongue first!

An albino lobster was caught by
Michael Farlin off Fubey and taken
to the North Yorkshire aquarium in
November 1997. He was named Barry
and was then kept carefully since he
was very valuable. Another albino, ten
centimetres smaller, called Lionel, had
been sold in the USA for £14,000.

 Ramu the killer whale, who was moved
from England to California because
he was too big to keep, grew at a
tremendous rate. Aged ten, he ate 386 kg
of fish a day and weighed 3.4 tonnes.

 The 30-centimetre leafy seadragon,
a relative of the sea horse, looks like
a piece of seaweed.

Life can exist in the strangest places. Deep in the ocean off Mexico, eyeless worms live in methane ice. Both the worms and the ice were discovered as recently as 1997.

 A killer whale was once harpooned by a fisherman off Long Island, USA. The fisherman and his crew were astounded when the whale broke free and turned to follow the boat. Despite the terror of the crew, the whale made no attempt to attack.

 The first underwater photos were taken by Louis Boutan of France in a bay off the French coast in 1893.

 Aquatic animals like penguins are short-sighted when out of water.

On 13 January 1852, the crew aboard the whaler *Monongahela* set out from New Bedford, Massachusetts, under the command of Captain Amos Seabury. Not far from Panama, they sighted another US whaler, the *Rebecca Sims*, and soon afterwards the lookout saw a strange shape in the water. Three boats were sent from the *Monongahela*. A huge head on a long neck emerged from the sea – it was twice as big as a whale.

After one boat was wrecked by the creature, the beast was harpooned. A towline was attached to it and the two whalers began hauling it in. Before long the monster died and the whole body floated to the surface. It was 100 metres long with a circumference of about 15 metres. The experienced sailors later described it as similar to a huge alligator. There was no chance of bringing the whole body on board, so the head alone was kept and pickled aboard the *Monongahela*.

Soon afterwards the two whalers

separated – the *Rebecca Sims* headed for home, while the *Monongahela* and its unique cargo set off for the Arctic. The *Monongahela* was not seen again. About ten years later a party of eskimos off Alaska found the only trace – the nameplate of the doomed ship. What the creature was remains a mystery.

 The man who introduced the hard hat for deep-sea diving was Augustus Siebe. It was in use by 1837 and made it possible for a person to move around fairly freely on the bottom of the sea.

 The armour-plated Chiton mollusc can live up to four kilometres below the surface of the ocean. It has up to 11,500 eyes!

The Great Barrier Reef, off the east coast of Australia, is the longest coral reef in the world, extending for over 2,000 kilometres.

 Conger eels can be up to 2.5 metres long and can weigh over 330 kg. Thousands of conger eels appeared on the surface of the sea off St Leonard's in Sussex during a very cold spell in January and February 1855. Nearly 80 tonnes were caught!

 Great treasures have been discovered in wrecks. In 1955 Teddy Tucker of the USA discovered a magnificent emerald-studded gold cross in a wreck of a Spanish galleon off Bermuda.

When John Allen and Gladys Moore married in 1927, Allen's father had a submarine built for them so they could spend most of their honeymoon underwater in the Caribbean!

 The cowrie shell was used as cash throughout the tropics up to this century. Some businessmen in England made a good trade out of collecting them, bringing them to England, then sending them to countries which used them as currency.

 In 1973 US diver and photographer Bill Curtsinger was attacked by a grey reef shark in the Caroline Islands. He said the bites were like sledgehammers and tore into his left hand and right shoulder. He was rescued by a friend in a dinghy.

In February 1948 an SOS was sent from a Dutch freighter, the *Ourang Medan*, which was in the Pacific on its way to Indonesia. The message said: 'Captain and all officers aboard dead. Entire crew dead or dying.' When rescuers reached the ship, they found all the officers in the chart room. All were dead – it seemed they had died within seconds of one another. Their eyes stared in horror and their arms were set, pointing upwards! On deck, dead men lay where they had fallen. There was no sign of disease, asphyxiation or poison on the bodies. What caused this sudden wave of death aboard the ship remains unknown.

 The tiger shark has a huge appetite. A four-metre-long shark was able to eat half a two-metre-long grey reef shark in one bite!

The remora, or sucker fish, has a sucker on top of its head, which it attaches to a shark or whale. The fish then eats the leftovers from the host. Sometimes the remora can end up in the shark or whale's mouth, where it will wait for food to come along.

 The swordfish can travel at up to 60 miles an hour (96 kph).

 Shark skin was once used as sandpaper.

 It is thought that nearly ten billion tonnes of gold lie at the bottom of the oceans, but in specks so small that it is not possible to mine.

The sack-throated whip-tail fish is among those that live at great depth. It is up to 60 centimetres long and has a thin tail like a whip which is up to 150 centimetres long. Its stomach is able to stretch to very large proportions; it is quite able to eat fish bigger than itself.

 Peter Benchley, the American writer, heard a story of a great white shark off Nantucket. In June 1971 he came up with the idea of a story called *Jaws*, his first book. He sold the film rights for $175,000. The film *Jaws* became the first film to gross over $100 million in the USA. The plastic sharks in the movie weighed 1.5 tonnes, cost $150,000 and were all called Bruce.

 The Bermuda Triangle is also known as the Triangle of Death, the Devil's Triangle and the Hoodoo Sea.

Auguste Piccard, the famous Swiss explorer, and his identical twin, Jacques, descended to 3.5 kilometres under the sea in 1960. Jacques later went down 11 kilometres into the Mariana Trench in the Pacific. Auguste became the model for Professor Calculus in the Tintin books.

 The eyes of a blue whale are six times wider than those of a human.

 The whale shark is harmless – it feeds on plankton.

In 1956, at the Australian swimming championships, before he went into the pool, Gary Winram was hypnotized to believe he was being chased by a shark! He still only came second.

 Unlike most fishes, whales and sharks cannot swim backwards.

 The eggs of a sea horse hatch inside a pocket on the father's belly. A sea horse can move each eye in a different direction at the same time.

 Penguins can swim fast enough underwater to allow them to leap two metres or more into the air and on to land or ice.

Adult dolphins are said to have a mental age equivalent to that of a seven-year-old child.

 After the world fishing exhibition at Vigo, Spain, in 1973, thousands of dead fish suddenly appeared in the harbour. They had been killed by the detergent used to clean up the exhibition site.

 The octopus has three hearts.

 The world's largest crab is found in deep seas off Japan. It is known as the Japanese spider crab and it has the largest leg span of any arthropod, reaching up to 3.8 metres (12 feet) across! It can live for up to 100 years.

In 1997 the international trade in seaweed was worth £2.3 billion!

 The first submarine, the *Turtle*, was built by an American, David Bushnell, in 1776. It was used in the American War of Independence and was the first vessel to use a propeller.

 One of the most unusual underwater explorers is the dog Hooch, owned by Sean Herbert. Hooch first went into the sea when she followed her master one day – and liked it. Over a few years Hooch became a real explorer. Sean bought her her own £700 scuba outfit and she made 14 underwater dives! Hooch also took to the air, making 53 parachute jumps. She had to retire when she broke her leg – jumping off her master's bed!

It was once found that the octopuses in Monterey Bay, California, were finding new places to live – they were making homes in beer cans which had been thrown away.

 Squid communicate with each other by changing colour.

 Each dolphin has its own whistle. Angry dolphins can make noises loud enough to kill nearby fish.

 Humpback whales can be heard at a distance of 1,200 kilometres – the distance between London and Barcelona, Spain.

An unknown creature attacked the *Stein*, a US frigate, off California. It left behind hundreds of pointed teeth embedded in the rubber coating that protected the radar apparatus below the waterline.

 There are said to be more wrecks off the coast of South Africa than anywhere else. One of the stretches of this forbidding area is known as the Skeleton Coast, for good reason.

 Native divers in the Pacific will dive to depths of up to 37 metres – the height of a 14-storey building – for pearls. The pressure at this depth is up to five times that of the pressure on land. The divers can stay down for about three minutes.

During a trip in 1966, the *San Pueblo*, a US Navy research vessel, came across an awesome sight off Newfoundland, Canada. A sperm whale, some 18 metres long, was throwing itself out of the sea in an attempt to escape the tentacles of a giant squid said to be just as long!

 In 1976 the US navy vessel the *AFB14* caught an unknown shark. It was 4.5 metres long and weighed three quarters of a tonne. It had seven rows of needle-like teeth. Because of its huge jaws it was named Megamouth.

 When young, a barnacle has three pairs of legs and one eye. It becomes even stranger as it gets older – gaining another eye and two more legs and then losing its mouth!

Experiments show that the squid is attracted by the colour red. It seems that many of the survivors from ships sunk in World War II were doomed because they wore bright red life jackets.

 Somewhere in the Indian Ocean, 5,000 humpback whales gather together and breed. The exact location is kept a secret so that the whales are not disturbed by visitors or tourists.

 The giant squid is the largest living creature without a backbone.

 The starfish is the only animal able to turn its stomach inside out.

The gannet, a large seabird, eats so much that it is sometimes unable to fly.

 Gary Smart, of Billy Smart's circus, was given two weeks' leave from the army because a killer whale was missing him at home.

 In 1983 a company in Ohio began making two artificial flippers for a 770-kg, 50-year-old turtle named Lucky, after she had been in a battle with a shark. After spending $20,000 on research, the operation was performed in January 1984.

 Britain's oldest bird, a Manx shearwater, was first ringed in May 1957 when it was six years old. As of 2003 it was 55 years old.

The Mae West was an inflatable rubber and canvas life vest issued to Allied airmen in World War II. It was named after the famous US film actress.

Two thirds of the world's 5.5 billion people live within 50 miles or 80 kilometres of the sea.

The bottom of the ocean remains the most unexplored area of the world – so far only about 1.5 per cent of the seabed has been looked at in detail.

The bottle-nosed dolphin has superb hearing. It can detect sounds at a higher pitch than the radar of bats.

The liver of a shark can be up to 10 per cent of its total weight.

 King penguins are said to fall backwards in surprise on seeing humans.

 Spiny lobsters walk on the seabed one after another, tail to antenna. They can travel at a speed of 35 centimetres a second.

 In 1796 the Lord Mayor of London was Brook Watson. He was unusual since he had lost a foot to a shark in the harbour of Havana, Cuba.

 The deepest life form isn't in the sea, or even at the bottom of the sea, but under the floor of the sea! A type of bacteria has been found 842 metres below the seabed in the Woodlark Basin in the Pacific Ocean off New Guinea!